CHEMICAL CHANGES

LYNNETTE
BRENT

D1625481

Crabtree Publishing Company

www.crabtreebooks.com

Crabtree Publishing Company
www.crabtreebooks.com

Author: Lynnette Brent
Coordinating editor: Chester Fisher
Series editor: Scholastic Ventures
Project manager: Santosh Vasudevan (Q2AMEDIA)
Art direction: Dibakar Acharjee (Q2AMEDIA)
Cover design: Ranjan Singh (Q2AMEDIA)
Design: Ruchi Sharma (Q2AMEDIA)
Photo research: Ekta Sharma (Q2AMEDIA)
Editor: Adrianna Morganelli
Project editor: Robert Walker
Production coordinator: Katherine Kantor
Font management: Mike Golka
Prepress technicians:
Katherine Kantor, Samara Parent, Ken Wright

Photographs:
Cover: Sam DCruz/Shutterstock; Title page: Andersen Ross/Jupiter Images;
P4: Witold Ryka/Istockphoto; P5: Perry Harmon/Istockphoto (left);
P5: Rodiks/Dreamstime (right); P6: Fanelie Rosier/Istockphoto; P7: David
Coder/Istockphoto (top); P7: Derek Thomas/Shutterstock (bottom);
P8: Clayton Hansen/Istockphoto; P9: Kuznetsov Dmitriy/Shutterstock;
P10: Lucwa/Istockphoto; P11: Alm/Photolibrary (top); P11: Andrey
Chmelyov/Istockphoto (bottom); P12: Oneclearvision/Istockphoto;
P13: Steven Gibson/Istockphoto (top); P13: Greg Nicholas/Istockphoto
(bottom); P14: Socrates/Dreamstime; P15: Zmaj011/Dreamstime (top left);
P15: Liza McCorkle/Istockphoto (bottom right); P16: Nicholas Piccillo/
Fotolia; P17: Terex/Fotolia (top); P17: Wade H. Massie/Shutterstock
(bottom); P18: Joel Blit/Istockphoto; P19: Michiel de Boer/Istockphoto;
P20: Thomas Christie/Fotolia; P21: Arni Katz/Alamy; P22: Ingram
Publishing/Photolibrary; P23: Pixelmaniak/Istockphoto (top); P23: IRC/
Fotolia (bottom); P24: Vaida/BigStockPhoto; P25: Gelpi/Shutterstock;
P26: Diane N. Ennis/Shutterstock; P27: Image Source Black/Jupiter
Images (top); P27: Zina Seletskaya/Shutterstock (bottom); P28: Darla/
BigStockPhoto; P29: Christoph Weihs/Istockphoto (top); P29: Norman
Chan/Fotolia (bottom)

Illustrations:
Q2A Media Art Bank: P5

Library and Archives Canada Cataloguing in Publication

Brent, Lynnette, 1974-
    Chemical changes / Lynnette Brent.

(Why chemistry matters)
Includes index.
ISBN 978-0-7787-4241-8 (bound).--ISBN 978-0-7787-4248-7 (pbk.)

    1. Chemical reactions--Juvenile literature. 2. Chemistry--Juvenile
literature. I. Title. II. Series.

QD501.B74 2008   j541'.39   C2008-903499-6

Library of Congress Cataloging-in-Publication Data

Brent, Lynnette, 1974-
    Chemical changes / Lynnette Brent.
        p. cm. -- (Why chemistry matters)
    Includes index.
    ISBN-13: 978-0-7787-4248-7 (pbk. : alk. paper)
    ISBN-10: 0-7787-4248-2 (pbk. : alk. paper)
    ISBN-13: 978-0-7787-4241-8 (reinforced library binding : alk. paper)
    ISBN-10: 0-7787-4241-5 (reinforced library binding : alk. paper)
    1. Chemical reactions--Juvenile literature. 2. Chemistry--Juvenile literature.
I. Title. II. Series.

QD501.B7924 2009
541'.39--dc22
                                                                    2008023542

Crabtree Publishing Company
www.crabtreebooks.com   1-800-387-7650

Published in Canada
Crabtree Publishing
616 Welland Ave.
St. Catharines, ON
L2M 5V6

Published in the United States
Crabtree Publishing
PMB16A
350 Fifth Ave., Suite 3308
New York, NY 10118

Published in the United Kingdom
Crabtree Publishing
White Cross Mills
High Town, Lancaster
LA1 4XS

Published in Australia
Crabtree Publishing
386 Mt. Alexander Rd.
Ascot Vale (Melbourne)
VIC 3032

Contents

Chemical Reactions

What is a **chemical reaction**? You have seen them, but you might not know they are reactions! When a steel garbage can **rusts**, you have a chemical reaction. The chemicals that react are iron and chemicals in the air. Water forms because of a chemical reaction. If hydrogen gas and oxygen gas were alone together for a long time, they would make water. Want to make the reaction happen more quickly? Add a little spark of fire, and you end up with an explosion! Water would form during this explosion.

A chemical reaction makes something happen, like rust or water. To make a reaction, two or more **atoms**, **ions**, or **molecules** need to touch. What are these parts, exactly? Atoms are the smallest parts of an **element** that have the element's **properties**. Imagine that a big group of gumballs is an element. If you had just one gumball, it would have the same properties as the other gumballs. A single gumball is kind of like an atom.

Physical and Chemical Reactions

A chemical reaction makes something new. When hydrogen and oxygen combine, they make something different from each part: water. In a physical reaction, the original material stays the same. If you freeze water, you create ice. The water is still there, it is just in a different state. If you heat the ice, you will have liquid water again.

When butter melts, it looks different, but it is still the same material. The change is a **physical change.**

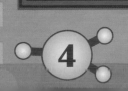

Breaking glass creates a physical change. The glass is still the same material after it has broken.

A molecule is made of two or more atoms. An ion is a special kind of atom. An atom has three parts—neutrons, protons, and electrons. If an atom has more of one part than the other two, the atom becomes an ion.

No matter whether the reaction involves atoms, molecules, or ions, a change must take place for a reaction to be a chemical reaction. One kind of material has to turn into something else.

Once you burn leaves, you cannot get the leaves back in their original forms. Leaf burning is a chemical change.

How Chemicals React

In any chemical reaction, there is a change. The substances change, and the substances could get hotter or colder. But **matter** and energy in a chemical reaction are not created or destroyed. The matter and the energy are the same before and after a reaction.

In a **synthesis reaction**, two substances combine. The two substances make a new, different, more complex compound. This means that the product has more atoms.

A **decomposition reaction** is the opposite of a synthesis reaction. A substance breaks down into parts. The parts left over after the reaction are different from the original substance.

Chemical Changes: Indicators

*These **indicators** show chemical reactions.*
Light: Imagine fireworks bursting. Their light indicates a reaction.
Heat: Heat can be released or absorbed. Chemicals in cake batter react during cooking because of heat.
Gas formation: Drop antacid into water. See the bubbles? They are a gas.
Precipitate: When a solid comes from a liquid during a reaction, it is called a precipitate.
Change in color: Have you seen a leaf change color? That is an indicator!

The forming of bubbles shows that a chemical change has taken place rather than a physical change.

When a penny turns green, the copper goes through an oxidation reaction. The reaction takes a long time.

Oxidation is a reaction between oxygen and any substance that reacts with oxygen. Rust is probably the best-known oxidation reaction, but not all materials that interact with oxygen turn to rust.

Reduction is a reaction that occurs at the same time as oxidation. When one material is oxidized, it gains some of those small parts of atoms and electrons. Matter is not lost in a chemical reaction, so those electrons had to come from somewhere! One of the reacting chemicals had to lose some of its electrons to the other material.

Scientists use safety equipment when they work with reacting chemicals. Some chemical reactions are violent, so be careful!

Synthesis

The word synthesize means to create or to make something new. This word perfectly describes a certain kind of chemical reaction. In a synthesis reaction, two substances combine. The combination creates something new.

One substance that is part of your life every day is water. A synthesis reaction creates water. Two hydrogen atoms combined with one oxygen atom make water, otherwise known as H_2O. The 2 shows that there are two hydrogen atoms for every atom of oxygen in water. In a glass of water, there are many, many groups of these three atoms. Remember, atoms are very tiny!

Another synthesis reaction makes a certain kind of acid. An acid is a substance that can taste sour and can react with other materials to make salts. One acid you may already know is lemon juice. There are other, more potent acids as well. If you were to combine water and a substance called sulfur trioxide, the chemical reaction would make sulfuric acid.

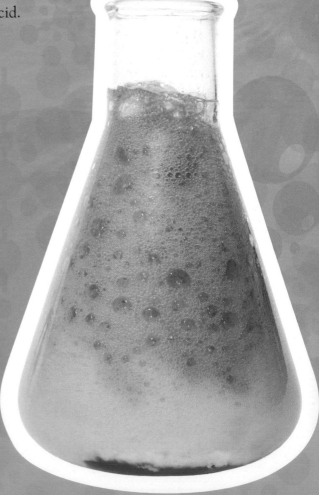

Make a Water Molecule!

You can show what happens in a synthesis reaction. Cut out small circles from red paper. Label each piece of paper with an H. Cut out larger circles of blue paper. Label each piece of paper with an O. Use your "hydrogen atoms" and "oxygen atoms" to show water. Attach two H circles to one O circle. You now have a model of water.

Scientists often use easy-to-find materials to make models. Besides paper, what other materials could you use to make "water"?

One important thing to know about synthesis reactions is that the two substances combine and only create one thing. If there were more than one product, the reaction could not be a synthesis reaction. If you were witnessing a synthesis reaction in a chemistry lab, what would you see? You would see two materials combine. A single new material would appear.

Water is a product of a synthesis reaction. Depending on the temperature, water can be a solid, a liquid, or a gas.

Decomposition

Decomposition is the opposite of synthesis. In synthesis, substances come together and create something new. When things decompose, they come apart. In a decomposition reaction, one substance comes apart to make two or more substances. These substances have chemical names. The substance that comes apart is a **reactant**. A reactant is the starting substance in any chemical reaction. The other substances in the reaction are **products**. Every chemical reaction forms products.

A synthesis reaction creates only one product. Decomposition reactions can form more than one product. But a decomposition always has only one reactant. In many decomposition reactions, heating a liquid or a solid reactant forms liquid and gas reactants. One important thing to know about decomposition reactions is that some of them need a "jump start" to get going.

Changes in temperature often cause decomposition reactions. Heat from the Sun can cause many decomposition reactions.

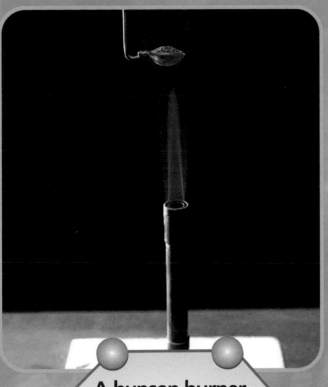

Very few decomposition reactions happen from a reactant just left on its own to decompose. Instead, the surroundings of the reactant need to change. Often, heating a reactant creates the decomposition reaction.

If you witnessed a decomposition reaction in a lab, what would you see? Most likely, you would see a substance in a test tube being heated. The single material in the test tube would come apart into more than one material. One of the materials might be an invisible gas. When scientists heat substances, they use safety devices to "capture" the gases.

A bunsen burner is a tool used to heat substances in a lab. Be very careful with heat.

Why Does Soda Lose Its Fizz?

When you shake a bottle of soda and then open it, you might notice that soda will soon lose its "fizz." Why does this happen? You are witnessing a decomposition reaction. The reactant is carbonic acid. That carbonic acid decomposes into carbon dioxide and water. Remember that "jump start?" Shaking the bottle makes the decomposition happen more quickly.

Do you want your soda to keep its bubbles? Don't shake it! Once the gases are gone, they are gone for good.

What is Oxidation?

You notice that the fender on the old bike in the garage is covered with **rust**. You cut an apple, leave it out on the counter, and it turns brown. Copper pennies can turn green over time. What causes these changes? A chemical reaction, oxidation, creates them all.

In an oxidation reaction, oxygen molecules react with different substances they may come into contact with. The substances could be metal, like the bike fender, or living tissue, like the apple. Oxidation can have positive effects. An oxidation reaction makes aluminum, a material that people use for many useful things, especially in the kitchen. (Aluminum pans are great for baking pizza!)

Oxidation can be negative as well, causing things like rusted automobiles and spoiled fruit. How does oxidation happen? With iron, the oxygen actually makes a slow burning process. As the iron slowly burns, rust forms. With copper in pennies, the oxygen causes a greenish coating. The penny is not weaker, it just looks different.

How can you control oxidation? Oxidation depends on the amount of oxygen in the air and the material the air touches. The best protection against oxidation is some kind of **coating**. When you get an apple from the store, the apple does not spoil unless the skin is broken. One tiny break in the skin makes an opening for oxygen. That break can soon become a "brown spot." The technical name for that brown spot? Oxidation!

Oxidation makes rust on iron. This oxidation happens slowly over time.

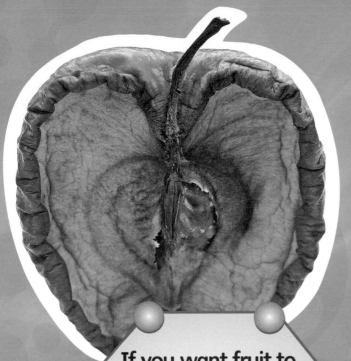

If you want fruit to stay fresh, leave skins on as long as you can. Once cut, oxygen causes browning.

Why Doesn't it Rust?

Stainless steel is a combination of different metals and substances, such as chromium, nickel, and nitrogen. These steels resist rust because they have barriers that prevent oxygen from affecting the metal. Stainless steel helps buildings last and makes materials safe for cooking. If you paint plain steel, oxygen can get through the paint and make rust. Stainless steel will never oxidize.

The outer layers of paint on a car are exposed to oxygen in air and water. Waxing the car prevents rust.

What is Reduction?

Oxidation often has a partner—reduction. Think about our rusty bicycle fender. The element iron reacted with oxygen to create rust. What could you do to take the rust away? If you could somehow remove the oxygen, the metal would go back to its pure form. That reaction would be reduction.

Oxidation and reduction play a large part in our everyday lives. Imagine that you have a brightly colored shirt, and you want the shirt to fade so it is not quite so bright. Long ago, you would simply leave a colored cloth out in the sun and air. (This still works; it just takes a while.) Bleaches do the job much more quickly. They use oxidation/reduction reactions to fade fabrics. The bleach introduces oxygen to the fabric, so the fabric is oxidized. The more oxidation occurs, the more the fabric fades. The bleach is reduced during the reaction. The bleach loses oxygen.

Have you ever stood near a bonfire to keep warm? The heat of a bonfire is caused by an oxidation/reduction reaction.

Oxidation and Reduction in Our Bodies

Many chemical reactions happen inside our bodies. Sugar in our bodies can be converted into energy. This process is an oxidation/reduction reaction. Glucose, or sugar, is oxidized. The carbon in glucose changes to carbon dioxide during the oxidation. When this happens, heat is released. That heat is energy—it helps us move!

An oxidation/reduction reaction takes place inside a combustion engine.

Oxidation and reduction help us get instant energy from sugary foods. The energy is "quick" though. The energy goes away after the reaction.

The burning of fuels, called **combustion**, is a common example of oxidation and reduction. Propane is a fuel that people can use for cooking. When propane burns in air, its carbon atoms are oxidized to make a gas. Then the oxygen is reduced to form water. The result of the reaction is useful heat!

Precipitation

A precipitate is a solid that forms out of a solution. To think about precipitates, you need to learn two new words: **soluble** and **insoluble**. If something is soluble in a substance, it can dissolve. Something insoluble will not dissolve. If you put sugar in water, for example, the sugar will dissolve. You say the sugar is soluble in water. If you put dirt in water, the dirt will not dissolve. So dirt is insoluble in water.

The materials at the bottom of a stream are not precipitates. Chemical reactions did not create them. Rushing waters simply deposited these materials.

In some chemical reactions, a precipitate forms because the precipitate is not soluble in the solution. Imagine a chemist mixing a liquid and a solid. You already know that a chemical reaction creates new substances, so parts from the liquid combine to make a new liquid. A solid might form, too. If the solid is insoluble in the liquid, it creates a precipitate. Precipitation reactions occur all around us.

The pipes in our homes can become clogged when the water reacts to substances in the pipes, making a precipitate. That precipitate can simply sit in the pipes and block the flow of water. A kidney stone, a hard deposit of materials inside the kidney, is a precipitate. It forms from calcium in the body. If you drink a lot of water, the precipitate becomes more soluble. Drinking a lot of water is one way to avoid kidney stones.

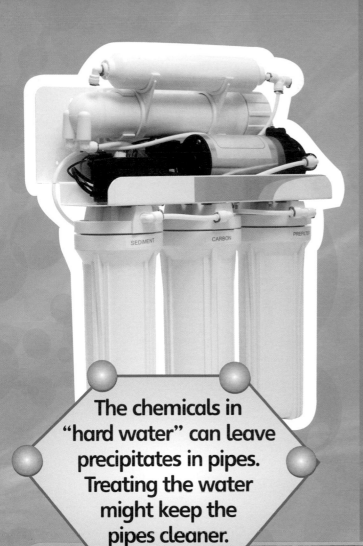

How Do People Use Precipitation?

Precipitation reactions help make our water safe to drink. In many cities, the water supply comes from rivers, streams, or lakes. This water on its own may contain all sorts of impurities that make the water unsafe. In a water treatment plant, solids are separated from the water. Then chemical reactions take even more precipitates out of the water.

The chemicals in "hard water" can leave precipitates in pipes. Treating the water might keep the pipes cleaner.

Wastewater treatment plants produce water safe to drink. Unsafe drinking water might still be used for jobs like watering golf courses.

Rates of Reaction

Different chemical reactions happen at different rates. You already know about rust. Rust develops slowly as metal is exposed to oxygen. Other reactions happen quickly! When you see fireworks, the explosion is a chemical reaction. That reaction happens very quickly, almost in an instant.

What makes some reactions happen more quickly than others? The **rate of a reaction** has another name: reaction kinetics. Kinetics is just another way to talk about how quickly or slowly a reaction happens. Several factors affect reaction kinetics.

One factor is **concentration**. Concentration is the amount of substance that is packed into the same space. A room with 100 people has a higher concentration than the same room with only 10 people in it. If the reactants have a high concentration, the reaction usually happens more quickly.

Catalysts

*A **catalyst** is a substance added to a chemical reaction to make it go more quickly. When the reaction is over, the same amount of catalyst is still there. When manufacturers make ammonia, a common cleaner, the reaction to make it happens much more quickly when iron is added to the reactants.*

Rust forms relatively slowly. People probably would not want a catalyst to make their items rust more quickly!

The chemical reaction that causes fireworks happens quickly. This reaction does not need a catalyst. Heat helps the reactants combine quickly to cause the explosion.

Another factor is temperature. Usually, if the temperature is higher, the reaction happens more quickly. That is why scientists often heat up reactants—the reaction happens more quickly that way. Scientists need to be careful, though. Once the temperature reaches a certain point, the reactions may slow down or actually stop.

Finally, medium is a factor in a chemical reaction. The medium is the substance in which the reaction takes place. Reactions take place in liquid, solids, or gases. Some reactions go more quickly in liquids, while other reactants have faster reactions if they take place in gases.

Reaction Energy

Energy is part of every chemical reaction. Matter and energy are not created or destroyed in a reaction. The reactants and the products are different, but they have the same amount of matter and the same amount of energy. Something that is hot has a lot of kinetic energy. It wants to give some of that energy away, so you feel heat. If something is cold, it does not have a lot of kinetic energy. It absorbs energy from its surroundings and feels cold.

Chemical reactions are classified two ways according to the heat they either produce or absorb. An **exothermic** reaction gives off heat. In a chemistry lab, an exothermic reaction can produce heat or may even be explosive. Think of those fireworks! Fireworks exploding are exothermic reactions.

An **endothermic** reaction needs heat for the reaction. These reactions have to absorb energy from the surroundings. These kinds of reactions cannot simply happen on their own.

Striking a match causes an exothermic reaction. Heat is instantly released by the reaction.

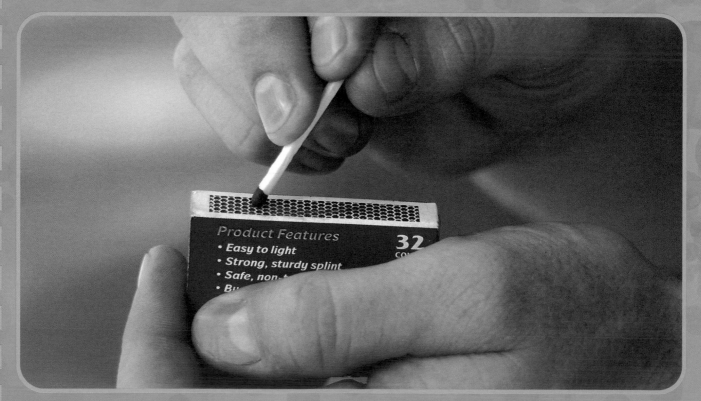

Product Features
• Easy to light
• Strong, sturdy splint
• Safe, non-
• Bu

32

Energy has to be added to the situation. The energy can come from heat in a lab. The energy can also come from the Sun.

You can do a safe exothermic experiment. Wrap a piece of steel wool around a thermometer. Measure its temperature. Then soak the piece of steel wool in vinegar for one minute. If you wrap the steel wool around the thermometer and leave it there for five minutes, you will notice a temperature change!

How Do Cold Packs Work?

An instant cold pack can bring relief to an injured athlete. You strike the cold pack on a hard surface and it becomes cold instantly. How does it work? A cold pack has two compartments. One compartment has a chemical, and the other has water. When the two mix, the chemical absorbs the water. The reaction is endothermic, so the cold pack absorbs heat and becomes cold.

A cold compress is based on an endothermic reaction. The chemical mixes with the water to instantly cool it.

When Fuels Burn

Reaction energy is the release or the absorption of heat in a chemical reaction. When heat is released, many things burn. What happens when fuels burn?

The burning of fuels makes it possible for us to stay warm in our homes during cold weather.

Coal is a fuel. It is also a reactant in a chemical reaction. One of the main "ingredients" in coal is carbon. When coal burns, the carbon reacts with oxygen in the air to make a gas, carbon dioxide. This reaction is also combustion because the coal burns. The reaction releases heat energy, so it is an exothermic reaction. Oxygen makes the coal burn, so this same reaction is also an oxidation reaction.

When coal and other fuels with carbon burn, you can see tiny particles of carbon released into the air as a product of the reaction. The particles are smoke. Too much of the smoke has negative effects. It can turn buildings black and make it hard for us to breathe. Our atmosphere traps carbon dioxide gases. You need some of these gases to help Earth stay warm. But if too many of these gases are trapped, then Earth can overheat. Some experts believe that the trapping of gases on Earth is causing global warming, making our planet warmer than it should be.

22

What is a Fossil Fuel?

Fossil fuels are sources of fuel found in the Earth's crust. Petroleum and coal are fossil fuels. Scientists believe that fossil fuels formed from the remains of dead plants and animals exposed to heat and pressure in Earth's crust over hundreds of millions of years. These fuels take a long time to form—that is why they are nonrenewable.

When coal burns, it releases carbon dioxide into Earth's atmosphere.

Oil produces petroleum, a fuel that occurs naturally, burns to create power, and is limited in its supply.

Some fuels also contain small amounts of a substance called sulphur. When sulphur burns, a gas called sulphur dioxide can dissolve in clouds and cause acid rain. Acid rain can kill trees, hurt fish, and damage buildings.

Plants and Animals

You may not realize it, but right now, as you sit and read, chemical reactions are happening inside your body. If you look outside at a flower garden, you are seeing different chemical reactions. Not all reactions take place with test tubes and labs. All that is needed for a reaction are reactants that will change when they are combined. These changes take place inside plants and animals all the time!

Photosynthesis is a chemical reaction that happens inside plants. In this reaction, carbon dioxide, water, and light from the Sun react. The reaction produces sugar. Sugar allows the plants to grow and develop flowers and fruit. The other product of photosynthesis is oxygen. Photosynthesis helps animals, too. The oxygen released from plants helps animals breathe.

The bright flowers on this plant are a result of photosynthesis. Photosynthesis uses carbon dioxide and water to create oxygen and sugars.

Metabolism is an entire collection of chemical reactions, not just one reaction. Metabolism is the group of reactions that gives living things their energy. These reactions take the food that you eat and turn it into the energy you need to think, to move, and to grow. Metabolism does not happen just when you eat, it happens all the time. If metabolic reactions in an organism stop, then the organism dies. When an animal eats a plant, the animal takes in the sugar the plant formed during photosynthesis. In metabolism, the body breaks down the sugar so that the energy can be released to all the parts of the body and used as fuel.

What are Enzymes?

Enzymes are special molecules found in the digestive system. When you eat, enzymes break down proteins into substances called amino acids. Enzymes take fat and break it down into fatty acids. Carbohydrates in food such as bread are broken down into simple sugars. Sugar, amino acids, and fatty acids are all sources of energy for the body.

All animals, whether tiny or large, use the process of metabolism to grow. Without these chemical reactions, life would stop.

Reactions Around Us

Chemical reactions have two parts: reactants and products. In a chemical reaction, matter and energy are not created or destroyed. Some chemical reactions make heat, and others use heat. Chemical reactions can move quickly or slowly.

Chemical reactions are part of the world around us! When you eat, chemical reactions take place in your body. When you use cleaning products, you are using solutions created by reactions. If you strike a match, start an engine, or use a battery, you create a chemical reaction. Take a look at some chemical reactions in our lives.

1 Cutting Onions

You can hold an onion in the store, and it does not make you cry. So what happens when you cut it that suddenly makes your eyes tear up? You probably guessed—it is a chemical reaction. Onions have oil that contains sulfur. Sulfur irritates our noses and our eyes. When the onion is whole, the sulfur is contained inside.

Boiled Eggs

Boiling eggs is a chemical reaction. Once the egg is boiled, it cannot change back to the way it was! An egg does not simply change on its own. What causes this change? Remember that one factor in reaction kinetics is heat. The heat introduced by your stove creates the chemical reaction that hardens the insides of the egg.

Once you cut the onion, another gas is released. That gas, combined with the sulfur, actually makes an acid, sulfuric acid. That acid irritates our eyes, and our eyes blink to keep themselves safe. Be careful when onions make you cry—if you rub your eyes, you will make it worse. That acid is on your fingers . . . and then even more can get into your already irritated eyes.

1

Cutting onions releases sulfuric acid that irritates our noses and our eyes.

Swimming Pools

You might think that the filter in a pool does all the work, but chemicals make pool water safe for swimming. Bacteria live in water. Those bacteria could make swimmers ill. If water has the wrong balance of chemicals, skin can become very irritated. So, how do chemical reactions work in pools? A substance that contains chlorine is put into the water. The reaction creates an acid that kills bacteria but will not hurt swimmers.

2

A fire extinguisher covers the fire with carbon dioxide, cutting off the oxygen that it needs to continue burning.

2 Fire Extinguishers

A fire is caused by a chemical reaction between oxygen in the atmosphere and some sort of fuel, like wood or gasoline. You can have wood and gasoline together, and they do not burst into flames. They need heat introduced to burn. Most fire extinguishers contain carbon dioxide. When carbon dioxide is introduced into the fire, the gas is heavier than oxygen. It takes the place of the oxygen around the burning fuel, and the fire goes out.

3 Instant Film

If you have ever wanted a picture in an instant, you may have used instant film. Instant film was invented in 1947. This invention was a huge success. It might seem like magic, but the images appear on the film because of chemical reactions. Film works by capturing light. The light activates chemicals and creates reactions on the film. If you took a picture on film, you would need to have that film developed with special chemicals. On instant film, everything you need to develop the picture is already on the film. All of the materials needed to create a chemical reaction are already on the film. Once the camera takes a picture, that film needs to be exposed to air. The air activates all the chemicals, and your picture "magically" appears.

3

4 Baking Bread

Many chemical reactions happen in the kitchen. Baking bread involves chemical reactions. When bakers make bread, they use yeast. Yeast reacts with sugar to create the products carbon dioxide and alcohol. During baking, the alcohol burns off. But the carbon dioxide gas is what gives bread its light and airy texture.

You probably never thought of your kitchen as a chemistry lab, but that shows you chemical reactions are all around us. When two substances combine and then change, you have a chemical reaction. Next time you have a sandwich, think about the chemical reactions that made the bread and digest your food. If you cook over a fire, think about the reactions that happen when fuel is burned. And when you enjoy a fireworks show, be sure to "ooh" and "aah" not just over the beautiful colors, but over the chemistry that created these sights.

4

Glossary

acid A compound that usually has a sour taste and turns blue litmus paper red

atom The smallest component of an element that has the chemical properties of the element

catalyst A substance that causes or makes a chemical reaction go more quickly without itself being affected

chemical reaction A process in which one or more substances are changed into others

coating A thin layer of something

combustion The act or process of burning

concentration The amount of dissolved substance contained in a unit of volume

decomposition reaction A reaction in which one substance separates into two or more substances

element A substance that cannot be separated into simpler substances

endothermic Having to do with a chemical change that absorbs heat

exothermic Having to do with a chemical change that releases heat

indicator Something that indicates, or shows a sign of something

insoluble Incapable of being dissolved

ion An electrically charged atom or group of atoms

matter The substance or substances of which any physical object consists or is composed of

molecule The smallest physical unit of an element or compound consisting of one or more like atoms in an element and two or more different atoms in a compound

oxidation A reaction in which an element is combined with oxygen

photosynthesis A process in plants in which carbohydrates are synthesized from carbon dioxide and water using light as an energy source

physical change A process that involves a change without altering the composition of a substance

precipitate To separate a substance in solid form from a solution; the solid substance that results

product A substance obtained from another substance through chemical change

property A quality or characteristic of something

rate of reaction How fast a reaction takes place

reactant A substance or compound used up in a chemical reaction

reduction The reaction that occurs with oxidation

rust Orange or red coating that occurs when iron is exposed to oxygen over a long period of time

soluble Able to be dissolved in a substance

synthesis reaction Reaction in which two reactants combine to make one new product

Index

Webfinder

http://www.chemtutor.com

http://www.chem4kids.com

http://www.physlink.com

http://www.chemguide.co.uk

http://www.bbc.co.uk/schools/ks3bitesize/science/chemistry